YOU ARE

NOT

NEGRO, BLACK, COLOURED, MORISCO, NOR AN AFRICAN SLAVE

© *2014 CALIFA MEDIA*®

By

Grand Sheik Brother Kudjo Adwo El
Moorish Science Temple of America
Subordinate Temple #5 – Toronto
Canaanland

Edited by
Sis. Tauheedah S. Najee-Ullah El
Moorish Science Temple California, Inc.

You Are Not Negro, Black, Coloured, Morisco Nor An African Slave

© 2014
Califa Media ®

Written by
Grand Sheik Kudjo Adwo El
Moorish Science Temple of America
Subordinate Temple #5 - Toronto
Canaanland

Edited by
Sis. Tauheedah S. Najee-Ullah El
Moorish Science Temple California, Inc.

ISBN: 978-1-7332805-7-0

All Rights Reserved. Without Prejudice. No Part Of This Book May Be Reproduced Or Transmitted In Any Form By Any Means, Electronic, Photocopying, Mechanical, Recording, Information Storage Or Retrieval System Unless For The Liberation Of Minds And Gaining Knowledge Of Self.

Califa Media™
Canaanland
A Moorish Guide Publishing Company
cmcanaanland@gmail.com

Table of Contents

Moorish American Prayer 1

I. Introduction 2

II. The Negro Label 4

III. How Did Moors Get Stuck With the Negro Label? 7

IV. The Coloured Label 11

V. The Boulé a.k.a. Talented Tenth 15

VI. The Black Label 20

VII. The Moor Status 23

Index 27

Works Cited 27

Other Titles Available from Califa Media® 31

Moorish American Prayer

ALLAH, the Father of the Universe, the Father of Love, Truth, Peace, Freedom and Justice. ALLAH is my protector, my guide, and my Salvation by night and by day, through His Holy Prophet DREW ALI (Amen)

I. Introduction

Prophet Noble Drew Ali brought to us a concept of Man Know Thyself that was beyond comprehension to Negro, Blacks and Coloured People of the early 1900's. If you have never heard of your Prophet Noble Drew Ali, it's because you have accepted the labels Negro Black and/or Coloured. One might ask, what did Prophet Noble Drew Ali teach unconscious Moors, incorrectly labeled Negro, Black, Coloured? He came to teach his people how to be themselves. One of our covenants as Moors is to uphold the words of the Prophet Noble Drew Ali, who came in our image, with our language, in our land to save us by teaching us to accept the Truth about our denationalization and theft of our birthrights. The first lesson we receive coming into this Divine and National Movement are the Constitution and By-Laws of the Moorish Science Temple of America. Act 6 specifically teaches:

With us all members must proclaim their nationality and we are teaching our people their nationality and their Divine Creed that they may know that they are a part and partial of this said government, and know that they are not Negroes, colored Folks, Black People or Ethiopians, because these names were given to slaves by slave holders in 1779 and lasted until 1865 during the time of slavery, but this is a new era of time now, and all members must proclaim their free national name to be recognized by the governments in which they live and the nations of the earth, this is the reason why Allah the Great God of the universe ordained Noble Drew Ali, the Prophet, to redeem his people from their sinful ways.

The Moorish Americans are the descendants of the ancient Moabites who inhabited the North Western and South Western shores of Africa.

(Noble Drew Ali, The Divine Constitution and ByLaws 1926)[1]

---

[1] Divine Constitution and Bylaws, Act 6.

II. The Negro Label

We must study to know our true selves. Most unconscious Moors willingly accept the label Negro/ negro without knowing what it means, its origin, and most importantly, my people fail to consider why Europeans applied this label to beings with high concentrations of Melanin and/or Carbon. What is the fascination with these imposed labels? Why have unconscious Moors been so quick to embrace that which they know nothing of? Most unconscious Moors will answer these questions without qualification and of the querent say, "They're racist"! Others will jump on the "race card" bandwagon and claim the labeling to be acts of prejudice or "They did it to take away the culture of black people during slavery". There are many keys/lessons/tablets brought to us by the Prophet to help save the burnt copper tone masses and wake them up from their sinful ways and statelessness. Whether we look at this matter from a domestic, national or international perspective, all jurisdictions recognize this violation of natural law.

> *With us all members must proclaim their nationality and we are teaching our people their nationality and their Divine Creed*
>
> Act 6, Divine Constitution and By-Laws (Noble Drew Ali, The Divine Constitution and ByLaws 1926).

We, the original Americans, obviously had no clue as to our Nationality and our Divine Creed if it had to be taught to us by our Prophet Noble Drew Ali. Our Nationality is a very important part of our search for Knowledge of Self that no Negro, Black, or coloured

Organization, Group, Association nor Nation has dealt with. Other than Noble Drew Ali through the Moorish Divine and National Movement in North America from 1913-1929, few of our so-called leaders have dared examine this issue.

Nationality has spiritual energy as a word: the letter combination N-A in the teachings of the Kabballah, represent stability, the first principle and the double virtue of recoiling on itself and spreading out. (Rashid n.d.) [2] N-A can be found in the cipher of Principles surrounding Nationality and other words. NAme, NAtional, NAture, NAtural, NAtive, NAzarene, NAtal, NAzareth, NAvel (NAv El), NAvy, NAvigate, NAutical, North America (N.A.), NAga, NApoleon (shot the nose off the Sphinx), NAïve, NArcotics (inducing sleep or stupor), NArrative (a story or description of actual or fictional events i.e. slave narratives).

> *"But this adventure of the Negro in the New World has been structured differently in the United States than in other parts of this hemisphere. In spite of his adaptability, his willingness, and his competence, in spite of his complete identification with the Moors of the United States, he is excluded and denied. A barrier has been drawn against the Negro"* (Tannenbaum 1992)[3]

In the above quote it clearly states that the Negro is a Moor and that he is still excluded and denied rights as a Negro. Most "black scholars" are quick to pull the race card and blame Europeans for their actions. The truth of the matter regarding the Negro problem is right

---

[2] *Symbols of the Kabbalah,* performed by A.A. Rashid,, n.d.

[3] Frank Tannenbaum, *Slave and Citizen The Negro in the Americas: The Classic Comparative Study* (Boston: Beacon Press, 1992).

in the above quote, Negroes are Moors that don't call themselves Moors. When the Negro starts to read and study he will see that it's not racism, it is misrepresentation on his part. He will see that it is not the Europeans' fault the Negro was put into slavery in the Americas, it was his, the Negro's abandonment of his own Moorish heritage and culture for the idol Gods of Europe, which assisted in his enslavement.

III. How Did Moors Get Stuck With the Negro Label?

"The institution of slavery, which had long since died out in the rest of Europe, had here, in the Iberian Peninsula, survived for a number of reasons, especially because of the continuing wars with the Moors, which lasted until the very year of the "discovery" of America, 1492." (Tannenbaum 1992).[4]

"Starting American history in 1492 in honour of Columbus was the beginning of deception and planted the thought that this is where it all began instead of where it ended! One minute earlier, December, 31, 1491 where the decree was made to Black a Moor out of His- story" (Gorham Bey and Rosser El 2000)[5]

Negro is a Spanish word that means black and the Spanish under the guise of Queen Isabella, King Ferdinand and Cardinal Ximenes were the ones who stripped the Moors of their culture, language, ceremonies, customs and even their names in 1501 AD. Moors who failed to submit to the now ruling power of Spain were exiled to North Africa and the Atlantis Islands or killed through the decree of Charles V in 1526 AD. Charles V also bribed many electors of the Roman Empire to name him the Holy Roman Emperor giving him rule over

---

[4] Ibid

[5] Edna Goram Bey and D. Rosser El, *Who Were the Negroes Before Slavery?* (Hyattsville, MD: Moorish Pub., 2000).

more countries than any other European monarch.

Those who were baptized into Christianity were termed Moriscos. These Moriscos made a final stand in 1570 to reclaim Granada, but were unsuccessful in their campaign. No less than 3 million Moors were banished between 1492 and 1600. During the rule of the Moors, Spain was the center of civilization in Europe, and to this day, mosques continue to stand as the foundation of Spanish churches. No other European country has ever come close to the 800 year legacy of the Moors in Spain.

> *"As a matter of fact, the Negro was never a slave. To conceive the design of enslaving an individual we must presuppose that he is free; the first act of enslaving is to deprive him of his liberty. This, the Negro, never had since the creation of man. The Negro is an ape; hence, his status in the Universe, his relation to Man, like that of every other animal, was fixed irrevocably by God in the Creation, and no act upon man's part, whether legislative, executive or judicial, can change it".* (Carroll 1900).[6]

The Negro status as an identity for Moors is a fiction to say the least based on the information presented thus far. One of the most proven, factual cases to date to pinpoint the fraud of unconscious Moors being labeled Negroes was the Dred Scott case brought in 1857. (Scott v. Sandford 1857)[7] In the Dred Scott case the United States Supreme Court ruled that descendants of Africans who were Negro slaves were not included or intended to be included under the word citizen, whether emancipated or not, and remained without rights or

---

[6] Charles Carroll, *The Negro a Beast or In the Image of God* (St. Louis: American Book and Bible House, 1900).

[7] *Scott v. Sandford*. 60 U.S. 393 (1856)

privileges except such as those which the government was willing to grant them.

Let's read that again:

In the Dred Scott case the United States Supreme Court ruled that descendants of Africans who were Negro slaves were not included or intended to be included under the word citizen, whether emancipated or not, and remained without rights or privileges except such as those which the government was willing to grant them. So, here it is, plain and simple as a matter of law. Descendants of Africans who were Negro slaves have no rights or privileges! Below is an excerpt of Justice Daniel's opinion on the case-

"Now the following are truths which a knowledge of the History of the world and particularly of our own country compels us to know-that the African negro race never have been acknowledged as belonging to the family of nations; that as amongst them there never has been known or recognized by the inhabitants of other countries anything partaking of the character of nationality, civil or political policy; that this race has been by all nations of Europe regarded as subjects of capture or purchase; as subjects of commerce or traffic; and that the introduction of that race into every section of this country was not as members of a civil or political society, but as property in the strictest sense of the term". (Scott v. Sandford 1857)[8]

The Supreme Court of the United States has never overturned this ruling so it stands at Law that Negroes can <u>never</u> be citizens and

---

[8] Ibid, 475

their introduction to the Americas was as property, not citizens. This is why the charge against Dred Scott was Plaintiff in Error—he brought his complaint before the court as "free slave," when slaves in general had no rights or privileges. He was misrepresenting himself to the court as 'Scott,' when his true Moorish title and identity in the Americas would have been El or Bey. Why have none of the 'black African scholars' used this information, this finding in law, to show the people that being a Moor is not a third party perspective opinion. It is a very clearly documented fact that Negroes are the misnomered Moors. The bigger question is, if Negroes are Moors, then what is a Negro?

" Negro Yavira Arabo-Troglodyte Niger– Negro Yavira Arabo and Troglodyte Niger were the ancient names given to the black chimpanzee monkey primate, by the Ancient Moabite peoples of Southwest Amexem, South Africa, South America. The Negroes/Troglodytes proliferated the South lands, past and present, and can be found, abundantly, around the Amazon River Valley of Southwest Africa/America and the surrounding areas". (Tarik Bey 2007)[9]

"None of us was 'lowed' to see a book of try to learn. They say we get smarter than they was if we learned anything. If you just looked like you wanted to read or write, ooohhh you gots a lickin or were sold!!!" (Proctor 1937)[10]

---

[9] *U.S. Nigger Industry I & II*, presented by Taj Tarik Bey (Trenton, NJ: R.V. Bey Publications, 2007).

[10] Jenny Proctor, Interview with Federal Writers' Project (Washington, DC: Works Progress Administration, 1937), p.2

IV. The Coloured Label

88. What does the word coloured mean?

Coloured means anything that has been painted, stained, varnished or dyed. (Noble Drew Ali, 101 Koran Questions for Moorish Americans 2014)[11]

COLOURED– Having colour. Often capital C designating a dark skinned people, especially Negroes. Distorted or bias as by irrelevant or incorrect information. (American Heritage Dictionary 1969)[12]

[13] COLOUR– Appearance, guise, semblance or *simulacrum*, as distinguished from that which is real. (Black 1957)

COLOUR OF AUTHORITY-That semblance or presumption of authority sustaining the acts of a public officer which is derived from his apparent title or from a writ or other process in his hands apparently valid and regular. (Black 1957)

COLOUR OF LAW - The appearance and semblance, without the substance, of legal right. (Black 1957)

COLOURABLE – That which has or gives color. That which is in appearance only, and not in reality, that which is purports to be. Counterfeit, feigned, having appearance of truth. (Black 1957)[14]

In the early 1900's the National Association for the Advancement of Coloured People (N.A.A.C.P.) was founded in order to attempt to prove that the Negro problem in the Union States was fixable by

---

[11] *101 Questionnaire*, p. 19

[12] *American Heritage Dictionary* (Boston: Houghton Mifflin, 1969).

[13] H.C. Black, *Black's Law Dictionary* 4th ed.(St. Paul, MN: West Publishing, 1957) p. 331.

[14] Ibid, 332

fighting racial discrimination. The purpose of this association was to vanquish American racial oppression and global anti "black" racism.

"Marxian philosophy is a true diagnosis of the situation in Europe in the middle of the 19th century despite some of its logical difficulties. But it must be modified in the United States of America and especially so far as the Negro group is concerned." (DuBois, Marxism and the Negro Problem 1933).[15]

"The matter of the various names given to these twenty-two million people with all colours of every race of the globe was European psychology. Thus he is separated from the illustrious history of his forefathers who were the founders of the first civilization of the Old World. This matter should be looked into with the hope of correcting it." (Noble Drew Ali, Allah's Temple: The New Moorish Literature n.d.).[16]

"These names have never been recognized by any TRUE American citizens of this day" (Noble Drew Ali, Divine Warning for the Nations 2014)[17]

---

[15] W.E.B. DuBois, "Marxism and the Negro Problem," *The Crisis* 40 (May 1933): 103-104.

[16] Prophet Noble Drew Ali, "What Shall We Call Him?" *Allah's Temple: The New Moorish Literature*, http://moorishkingdom.tripod.com/id56.html, accessed 12 Dec., 2014.

[17] Prophet Noble Drew Ali, "Divine Warning for the Nations," *Moorish Jewels: Emerald Edition*, by G.S. Rami Salaam El, Sis. Tauheedah Najee-Ullah El, ed. (Redondo Beach, CA: Califa Media Publications, 2014), p. 16.

CIVILITER MORTUUS (Civil Death) – Civilly dead; dead in the eyes of the law. The condition of one who has lost his civil rights and capacities, and is accounted dead in the law. (Black 1957)[18]

"The problem of the twentieth century is the problem of the color line-the relation of the darker to the lighter races of men in Asia and Africa, in America and Islands of the seas". (DuBois, The Souls of Black Folk 1903).[19]

"The NAACP was created by two Jewish Brothers, Joel and Arthur Spingarn. The Jews or Zionist movement controls black policy and direction in America through their liberal unions such as, the American Civil Liberties Union, The American Jewish Committee, the Race Relations Department (under a variety of names) of the YMCA, YWCA, the American Friends Service Committee. The Rosenwald and Taconic Foundations, the National Council of Churches, The Ford and Rockefeller Foundations, The Roman Catholic Church, PUSH, The Leadership Conference on Civil Rights (LCCR), The National Urban League, The National Council of Negro Women, the A. Phillip Randolph Institute, The Congress of Racial Equality, and the Black Americans in Support of Israel Committee (BASIC). The Zionist movement has penetrated all black organizations. The Zionist movement uses Black Negro and Coloured organizations to get European

---

[18] Black, p. 313
[19] W.E.B. DuBois, *The Souls of Black Folk*, (Chicago: A.C. McClurg & Co., 1903), p. 210

flack away from themselves while quietly enhancing their economic domination of the world and their manipulation of the American presidency. W.E.B Dubois was appointed director of publicity and research for the NAACP". (Osahun 1993).[20]

---

[20] Naiwa Osahon, *God is Black,* (Berwyn Heights, MD: Heritage Books, 1993).

V. The Boulé a.k.a. Talented Tenth

"The most prestigious of all these black groups is the Boule, a fraternal organization founded in 1904, but many say that all these groups found their roots in the oldest surviving black fraternal men's organization, the Prince Hall Masons." (Graham, Our Kind of People: Inside America's Black Upper Class 1999).[21]

This is the foundation of the coloured race card game with unconscious Moors in North America. Many unconscious Moors didn't want to be affiliated with the Negro so instead engaged with the Europeans on a professional level. The integration of "black" men into "white" society created this coloured label. Majority of the "black upper class" were of mixed Moor and Melanin descent. The Boule are the black professionals who are deeply rooted and comfortable socializing and building a successful career among European businessmen and philanthropists. This integration is what created the coloured caste. The coloured label, in its early stages, was to distinguish between the nappy headed Negro slaves and the "good haired mixed bougie blacks". To further prove the wanting-ness of the elite "blacks" to be recognized, the Boule adopted the fraternal name Sigma Pi Phi but claim that it has no ties to Greek-Letter college fraternities. This is the same concept as Melanin beings calling themselves African but saying that has no connection to Scipio Africanus, the Roman General Africa is named after. To solidify the unification of the colonial masters

---

[21] Lawrence Otis Graham, *Our Kind of People*, (New York: Harper Perennial, 1999).

and the "black" elite, the British Grand Lodge gave Prince Hall permission to begin a "black version" of the organization and Prince Hall was given the title 'Most Worshipful Master'.

"The word Boule was used because it meant "council of Noblemen" or "senate". The members were each referred to as "archons" with the President known as "sire archon" and other officers taking Greek titles such as Grammateus, Thesauristes, Rhetoricus etc". (Graham, Our Kind of People: Inside America's Black Upper Class **1999**).[22]

The level of ignorance among our people is enough to have the world want to get rid of this Negro, Black, Coloured race of fictions. Just to begin to innerstand the severity of the brainwash, let's examine one of these Greek titles: Archon– One of the nine principal magistrates of Ancient Athens. Any of the various officials of the Byzantine Empire.

"According to Greek Mythology ZEUS, the "Father of the Gods" who is of Ethiopian ancestry (black), mates with the fair Greek maiden, Lo. The have a MULATTO son, Epaphus, born in Egypt" (Khamit-Kush **2000**)

It is a fact that Europeans feel more comfortable around less melanated people than they do around higher melanated people. Direct experience and observation has shown us that "light skinned

---

[22] Ibid.

blacks", as they are misrepresented, receive better job opportunities from European employers.

"Yes, these brothers that we are pushing up against the wall have taken a sworn oath that they will never expose the Europeans that they know that actuality runs the world." (Cokely n.d.).[23]

Alonzo Herndon was Atlanta's first "black" millionaire and his businesses included a twenty five seat men's barber salon that employed only "black" barbers and served only "white" businessmen. The essence of the Boulé is to fit into the European structure of society; to see what the most privileged "white" person has in life. The temptation to kill themselves as a melanin being was based on the misrepresentation of the Moor calling themselves "black" and thinking that their situations can be better if they "pass". The foundation of the Boulé is Ivy League educated yet unintelligent, unconscious Moors, thinking they need to "pass" for "whites" in order to receive some privileges from the occupying Inquisitionist of North America.

"Think of a manner in which to "kill" yourself off in the minds of Black people who know you and your family. If your family and siblings are willing participants in assisting you they can say that you now live outside the county, have entered a cult or have died. Develop associations with organizations and institutions that will buttress your resume. Convert to a Presbyterian Church or Republican (Whig) party. Contribute to charities like Daughters of the American Revolution. If your

---

[23] *The Boule (Sigma PiPhi): Advisors to the King,* presented by Steve Cokely.

physical appearance makes it possible, claim to be of White European background or darker European or Middle Eastern background. Never claim an ethnic group from Africa or America. Enhance those physical features that can support your new identity. Lightening your hair colour, narrowing your nose, thinning your lips, and adopting a more conservative style in clothing and speech are all simple steps that can aid your transition. Avoid sitting with or being photographed with black people because if you have any vaguely black features, those characteristics will be exaggerated and suddenly make you seem quite similar to "real blacks" standing near you. If members of your family you have divorced are willing to support your efforts in trying to pass, always meet them on neutral territory where neither you or they work, live or socialize. If the black relatives you have divorced are not willing to support your efforts, make a complete break from them, because they can too easily undo the façade you have created in your new community and new live. To avoid having a "throwback" child consider adopting white children." (Graham, Rules of Passing 2000)[24]

"I ran into her and confronted her at the airport several years ago, but the lies were so outrageous and so well-rehearsed that I couldn't get through to her. It absolutely amazes me how white people can't see the black in her. She even has the southern black twang. If she's gone through so much trouble to live in the white race, they can have her". (Graham, Rules of Passing 2000)

---

[24] Lawrence Otis Graham, "Rules of Passing," *The Social Construction of Race and Ethnicity in the United States*, Joan Ferrante ed., (Glenview, IL: Pearson, 2000).

ABANDONMENT – The giving up of a thing absolutely, without reference to any particular person or purpose, as throwing a jewel into the highway; leaving a thing to itself, as a vessel at sea; vacating property with the intention of never returning, so that it may be appropriated by another. (Black 1957).[25]

"What your ancient forefathers were, you are today without doubt or contradiction. There is no one who is able to change man from the descendant nature of his forefathers; unless his power extends beyond the great universal Creator Allah Himself." (Noble Drew Ali, The Holy Koran of the Moorish Science Temple of America Circle 7 1928).[26]

---

[25] Black, p.9.
[26] Chapter XLVIII, Verse 9-10 (HKMSTA).

VI. The Black Label

87. What is meant by the word black?
Black according to science means death. (Noble Drew Ali, 101 Koran Questions for Moorish Americans 2014)

The reason why we, as a community of Melanin beings, don't get it personally, financially or mentally is because we are in blackness. Blackness is the absence and absorption of light, light is knowledge scientifically. As Moorish Scientist all we can base anything truthfully are things in harmony with Science, which is described by Master Teacher Kaba Hiawatha Kamene as "seen spirituality." (Hiawatha Kamene n.d.)[27] The bold ignorance and hypocrisy of black people is why most of them have such extreme mental issues. The sell-out "black leaders" who taught and teach about Black History "sell" the Moorish history to the unconscious Moorish masses as a third party perception which is a violation of Truth to the common man and Nations of the Earth. Prophet Noble Drew Ali said you are not black because according to Nations of the world you have a Nationality. Modern Nation States have dealt with Noble Drew Ali's claim of nationality since his transition from this physical plane, so in actuality they are making these nationality claims in Human and Indigenous Peoples Declarations of right on his behalf. The ultimate reason why they made these International claims in his favour is because he came from North America and had a nationality what the European usurping colonizers took away to get these unconscious Moors in the racism jurisdiction.

---

[27] *Science is Seen Spirituality,* Presented by Kaba Hiawatha Kamene, n.d.

Article 6: Every indigenous individual has the right to a nationality.

Article 15: Everyone has a right to a nationality. No one shall be arbitrarily deprived of his nationality nor denied the right to change his nationality. (United Nations Declaration on the Rights of Indigenous Peoples 2007).

Black-a-Moor n. Any dark skinned person; especially an African negro. [Earlier More BLACK + More earlier form of Moor]. (American Heritage Dictionary 1969)

In no history books, earlier than the 17th century, do we see the word black, negro or coloured used in describing the burnt copper tone olive skinned Asiatics of the North America.

21. If a Citizen of the United States should kill or wound a Moor, or on the contrary if a Moor shall kill or wound a Citizen of the United States, the Law of the Country shall take place and equal Justice shall be rendered... (Treaty of Peace and Friendship, 1786 2008).[28]

> *"Through sin and disobedience every nation has suffered slavery, due to the fact that they honoured not the creed and principles of their forefathers. That is why the nationality of the Moors was taken away from them in 1774 and word, black and coloured was given to the Asiatics of America who were*

---

[28] *Treaty of Peace and Friendship 1786*, trans. Issac Cardoza Nunez. Yale Law School Lillian Goldman Law Library Avalon Project. Website http://avalon.law.yale.edu/18th_century/bar1786t.asp#art21 accessed 13 Dec. 2014.

of Moorish descent, because they honoured not the principles of their mother and father and strayed after the gods of Europe of whom they know nothing."- (Noble Drew Ali, The Holy Koran of the Moorish Science Temple of America Circle 7 1928).[29]

---
[29] *HKMSTA*, Chapter XLVII: V.16

VII. The Moor Status

Under the rule of the Moors between 711 and 1492, the people as a whole were content; as content as any people can be whose rulers are of a separate so called race and creed. The Moors under Prophet Noble Drew Ali's teachings know that Moors are the people of Humility. The charge of the Moors of Northwest Africa Amexem is to uplift fallen humanity. The time has come for Moors who have information to present this information. They are obliged to inform the masses and live out the legacy of our Ancient Foremothers and Forefathers who were the torchbearers of civilization.

Ancient Ones have returned in those active Moors who innerstand the metaphysical teachings of the Last Prophet with the saving power for Negro, Black, Coloured and African Moriscos out of their inferior status. Negroes, Blacks and Colored People are titles given to slaves during the time of slavery. The Moors are indigenous to North America and not Indians, Metis, Inuit or the other later forms of indigenous peoples in America. As persons from the Caribbean, for example, we must see the lies disguised as truth in order to raise ourselves from being labeled as the savages of humanity to our rightful place as Moors. What is Black, Negro and Coloured? **They are not recognized as nations**. The Forerunner Garvey said, "Europe cries to European, ho!/ Asiatics claim Asia, so/ Australia for Australians, and Africa for the Africans." (Garvey 1922). As Black, you are "soiled or stained with dirt, gloomy; pessimistic; dismal (a black outlook), deliberately; harmful; inexcusable (a black lie), boding ill; sullen or hostile; threatening (black words; black looks), without any moral quality or goodness (His black heart has concocted yet another black deed.), evil; wicked, indicating censure, disgrace, or liability to punishment, marked by disaster or misfortune, based on the grotesque, morbid, or unpleasant aspects of life (black comedy; black humor), and the list goes on and on. (American Heritage Dictionary 1969) As a "coloured" person, you are artificially produced; not natural, A Black person. (American Heritage Dictionary 1969). As a Negro you are a river in northwestern South America, flowing southeastern from eastern Colombia through northern Brazil into the Amazon; a river in southern Argentina, flowing east from the Andes to the Atlantic; a Black chimpanzee monkey called Negro Yavira Aribo.

> *"The inhabitants threw all their refuse into the drains in the center of the narrow streets. The stench must have been overwhelming, though it appears to have gone virtually unnoticed".* (Burke 1985).[30]

> *"They called themselves Moorish-Americans, and believed they were descended from Moors, or North Africans, who arrived on the American continent well before Christopher Columbus. At a time in history when terms like "Irish-American" and "Italian-American" had only begun to weave their way into the vernacular and the title "African-American" didn't exist, calling themselves "Moorish-Americans" offered a sense of identity absent in labels like*

---

[30] *The Day the Universe Changed*, written and performed by James Burke (United Kingdom: B.B.C., 1985), DVD.

"Negro". (G.S. Adwo El 2008).[31]

In 1928, Prophet Noble Drew Ali was a delegate to the Sixth Pan American Conference in Havana, Cuba. (Moon 2005).[32] This was an international conference of American Nations attended by dignitaries of North, South, and Central America. As the European Nations in these Indigenous lands of Moorish America are foreign occupiers, **hundreds of miles** out of their jurisdiction, they do not have claim to this land as this isn't Europe. Sheik Sharif Abdul Ali regained our inheritance of the land as he was the only Moorish representative, In Propria Persona, indigenous to these lands to receive the mandate for the land and acquiring the proper ownership of it through Trust Law. The only beneficiary, according to the land mandates, to this vast land trust are Moors through our Divine Prophet Noble Drew Ali, which makes us the successors or beneficiaries of the Trust who would inherit this estate once in Propia Persona Sui Juris.

"On the most obvious level it is from Giraldi Cinthio that Shakespeare gets the fact of his hero's darkness. Othello is a Moor, an African who has crossed the Mediterranean. Othello's darkness meant mystery to the Elizabethan; it also meant the unknown, the suppressed and unreasoned." (Rudzik 1966).[33]

---

[31] "How the 'Iron Sheik' brought a new faith to T.O," *The Globe and Mail*, Sep 20, 2008, national edition.

[32] Peter Moon, "The Ali Shuffle," *Montauk Book of the Dead* (New York: Sky Press 2005).

[33] O.H. Rudzik, introduction to *The Tragedy of Othello, The Moor of Venice*, by William Shakespeare (New York: Airmont Publishing Company Inc. 1966).

"The Moors, that is, the Arabs and Berbers occupied much of Spain and Portugal for seven centuries, and Arabs also held Sicily." (Coon 1965).[34]

"The end of Moorish Spain meant that the Moors ceased to exist as a nation, and became no more than a minority within a Christian country. The lesser status however they never accepted. On the estates of the nobles the Moors formed plentiful, cheap and productive source of labour from which the expression arose: Mientras mas Moros mas ganancia: "More Moors, more profit". Confiscations were meant in the first place fund the Inquisition during the expulsion of the Moors. It is reported that Ferdinand and

"Isabella divided all profits from confiscations into three sections, one for the war against the Moors, one for the Inquisition and one for pious purposes. The greatest part of the Spaniards, and especially those that count themselves as noblemen, are of the blood of the Moors." (Kamen 1965).[35]

---

[34] Carleton S. Coon and Edward E. Hunt Jr., *Living Races of Man*, (New York: Alfred A. Knopf, 1966).

[35] Henry Kamen, *Spanish Inquisition* (New York: New American Library, 1965).

Index

Amexem, 23

Ancient Ones, 23

archons, 16

Black-a-Moor, 21

bougie, 15

British Grand Lodge, 16

Cardinal Ximenes, 7

Carroll, Charles, 8

Charles V, 7

Cinthio, 25

coloured caste, 15

Columbus, 7

DuBois, W.E.B., 12, 13

Giraldi, 25

Granada, 8

Havana, Cuba, 25

Herndon, Alonzo, 17

Iberian Peninsula, 7

Inuit, 23

Kabballah, 5

King Ferdinand, 7

Metis, 23

Moriscos, 8

Othello, 25

Pan American Conference, 25

Plaintiff in Error, 9

Prince Hall Masons, 15

Queen Isabella, 7

Scipio Africanus, 15

Scott v. Sandford, 8

Shakespeare, 25

Sheik Sharif Abdul Ali, 25

Sigma Pi Phi, 15

Treaty of Peace and Friendship, 21

Trust Law, 25

Works Cited

American Heritage Dictionary. Boston: Houghton Mifflin, 1969.

Black, H.C. *Black's Law Dictionary*. 4th. St.Paul, MN: West Publishing, 1957.

Burke, James. *The Day the Universe Changed*. Directed by Richard Reisz. Performed by James Burke. 1985.

Carroll, Charles. *The Negro a Beast or In the Image of God*. St. Louis, MO: American Book and Bible House, 1900.

The Boule (Sigma Pi Phi): Advisors to the King. Performed by Steve Cokely. n.d.

Coon, Carleton S. and Edward E. Hunt, Jr. *The Living Races of Man*. New York: Alfred A. Knopf, 1965.

DuBois, W.E.B. "Marxism and the Negro Problem." *The Crisis*, May 1933: 103-104, 118.

—. *The Souls of Black Folk*. Chicago: A.C. McClurg & Co., 1903.

G.S. Adwo El, Kudjo, interview by Kate Hammer. *How the 'Iron Sheik' brought a new faith to T.O.* (Sep 20, 2008).

Garvey, Marcus. "Africa for the Africans." *Beverly M. Gordon College of Education and Human Ecology - Ohio State University*. 1922. http://u.osu.edu/gordon.3/files/2012/06/Appendix-VI1.pdf (accessed Dec 13, 2014).

Gorham Bey, E, and D. Rosser El. *Who Were The Negroes Before Slaves*. Hyattsville, MD: Moorish Pub, 2000.

Graham, Lawrence Otis. *Our Kind of People: Inside America's Black Upper Class.* New York: Harper Perennial, 1999.

Graham, Lawrence Otis. "Rules of Passing." In *The Social Construction of Race and Ethnicity in the United States*, by Joan Ferrante. Glenview, IL: Pearson, 2000.

Science is Seen, Spirituality is Unseen. Performed by Kaba Hiawatha Kamene. n.d.

Kamen, Henry. *Spanish Inquisition.* New York: New American Library, 1965.

Khamit-Kush, Indus. *What They Never Told You in History Class.* Vol. 1. Hunlock Creek, PA: EWorld Inc., 2000.

Moon, Peter. *Montauk Book of the Dead.* New York: Sky Books, 2005.

Noble Drew Ali, Prophet. "101 Koran Questions for Moorish Americans." In *"I'm Going to Repeat Myself.": A Collection of Artifacts Authored by the Prophet Noble Drew Ali & the M.S.T. of A.*, by Tauheedah S. Najee-Ullah El, 14-22. Redondo Beach, CA: Califa Media Publishing, 2014.

—. *Allah's Temple: The New Moorish Literature.* n.d. http://moorishkingdom.tripod.com/id56.html (accessed December 12, 2014).

Noble Drew Ali, Prophet. "Divine Warning for the Nations." In *Moorish Jewels: Emerald Edition*, by Rami A. G.S. Salaam El, 18. Redondo Beach, CA: Califa Media Publishing, 2014.

—. "The Divine Constitution and ByLaws." Chicago, Illinois: The Moorish Science Temple of America, Inc., 1926.

—. *The Holy Koran of the Moorish Science Temple of America Circle 7.*

Chicago: Moorish Guide Publishing, 1928.

Osahun, Naiwu. *God is Black*. Berwyn Heights, MD: Heritage Books, 1993.

Proctor, Jenny, interview by Works Progress Administration Federal Writers' Project. *Narrative of Jenny Proctor: Enslaved in Alabama 1850-1865* (1937).

Symbols of the Kabbalah. Performed by A.A. Rashid. n.d.

Rudzik, O.H. "Introduction." In *Tradgedy of Othello the Moor of Venice*, by William Shakespeare, 1. New York: Airmont Publishing Company Inc., 1966.

Scott v. Sandford. 60 U.S. 393 (1857) (The Supreme Court, 1857).

Tannenbaum, Frank. *Slave and Citizen: The Classic Comparative Study of Race Relations in the Americas*. Boston: Beacon Press, 1992.

Nigger Industry I & II. Performed by Taj Tarik Bey. R.V. Bey Publications, 2007.

"Treaty of Peace and Friendship, 1786." *Yale Law School-Lillian Goldman Law Library Avalon Project*. 2008. http://avalon.law.yale.edu/18th_century/bar1786t.asp#art21 (accessed Dec 13, 2014).

"United Nations Declaration on the Rights of Indigenous Peoples." *UN.org*. Sep 13, 2007. www.un.org/esa/socdev/unpfii/documents/DRIPS_en.pdf (accessed Dec 13, 2014).

Other Titles Available from Califa Media®

Moorish Children's Guide to History and Culture

Moorish Jewels: Emerald Ed

Moors in America

Moslem Girls' Training Guide a.k.a. The Sisters' Auxiliary Handbook

Nationality, the Order of the Day

Noble Drew Ali Plenipotentiaries

Official Proclamation of Real Moorish American Nationality

Well, Come to Klanada

Califa Uhuru Series

Vol. 1:   Holy Koran of the Moorish Holy Temple of Science, Circle 7

Vol. 2: "I'm Going to Repeat Myself.":   A Collection of Artifacts Authored by Noble Prophet Drew Ali and the M.S.T. of A.

Vol. 3:   Mysteries of the Silent Brotherhood of the East a.ka. The Red Book, a.k.a. Sincerity

Vol. 4:   Califa Uhuru; A Collection of Literature from the Moorish Science Temple of America

www.ingramcontent.com/pod-product-compliance
Lightning Source LLC
Chambersburg PA
CBHW060344080526
44584CB00013B/919